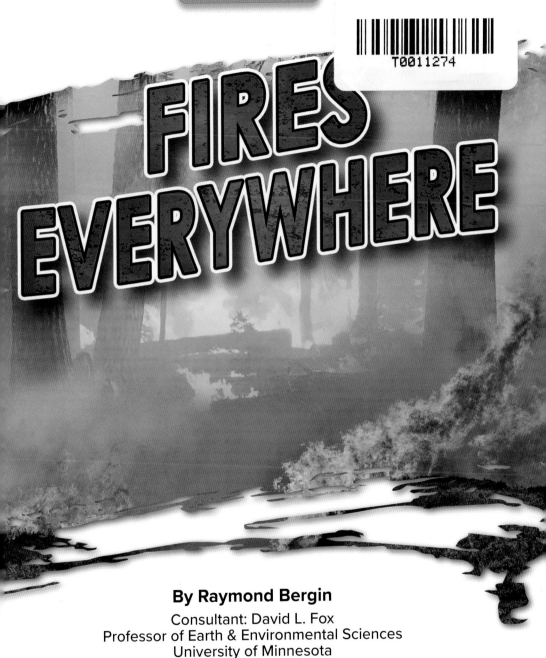

FIRES EVERYWHERE

By Raymond Bergin

Consultant: David L. Fox
Professor of Earth & Environmental Sciences
University of Minnesota

BEARPORT
PUBLISHING

Minneapolis, Minnesota

Credits

Cover and title page, © Stringer/Getty, © USFS Photo/Alamy; 4–5, © Binikins/ iStockphoto; 5, © eeqmcc/iStockphoto; 6–7, © Jorge Villalba/iStockphoto; 8–9, © NASA/ Wikimedia; 10–11, © benedek/iStockphoto; 12–13, © Perytskyy/Getty; 14–15, © Photos by Tai GinDa/Getty; 16–17, © My Photo Buddy/Shutterstock; 18–19, © Henrik_L/ iStockphoto; 20–21, © panaramka/iStockphoto; 22–23, © Andrew Kandel/Alamy; 24–25, © lovleah/Getty; 26–27, © Robert Wilder Jr/Shutterstock; 28, © skipro101/iStockphoto; 29, © Oleksandr Berezko/Shutterstock, © serts/iStockphoto, © Evgeniy Eivo/Shutterstock, © Wigandt/Shutterstock, © Creative Family/Shutterstock.

President: Jen Jenson
Director of Product Development: Spencer Brinker
Senior Editor: Allison Juda
Associate Editor: Charly Haley
Senior Designer: Colin O'Dea

Library of Congress Cataloging-in-Publication Data

Names: Bergin, Raymond, 1968- author.
Title: Fires everywhere / by Raymond Bergin.
Description: Minneapolis, Minnesota : Bearport Publishing Company, [2022] | Series: What on earth? climate change explained | Includes bibliographical references and index.
Identifiers: LCCN 2021039173 (print) | LCCN 2021039174 (ebook) | ISBN 9781636915562 (library binding) | ISBN 9781636915630 (paperback) | ISBN 9781636915708 (ebook)
Subjects: LCSH: Wildfires--Juvenile literature. | Climatic changes--Juvenile literature.
Classification: LCC SD421.23 .B47 2022 (print) | LCC SD421.23 (ebook) | DDC 363.37/9--dc23
LC record available at https://lccn.loc.gov/2021039173
LC ebook record available at https://lccn.loc.gov/2021039174

For more information, write to Bearport Publishing, 5357 Penn Avenue South, Minneapolis, MN 55419. Printed in the United States of America.

Contents

Up in Flames

The sun beats down on another hot summer day in southeastern Australia. **Billowing** black smoke suddenly appears in the distance above angry red-and-orange flames. A fast-moving fire is approaching. Dead trees and dry grasses catch fire and spur the flames forward.

Unusually hot and dry weather allowed thousands of wildfires to burn out of control in Australia during the summer of 2019 and 2020. What on Earth is going on?

In 2019 and 2020 alone, an area twice the size of Florida burned in southeastern Australia. As many as one out of every three koalas in that area were killed in the flames.

Burning Bigger

A wildfire is any unwanted or unexpected fire that spreads across wild land. Places that tend to be hot and dry have always had wildfires. Many of these places even have **fire seasons**—the times of year when fires are likely to happen. But in recent years, wildfires have broken out more often, grown larger, and burned longer. Even areas that normally don't face fire are being affected.

Why are fires burning more often and causing more damage? One of the biggest causes is a series of rising temperatures around the globe.

About 70,000 wildfires burn every year in the United States. The central, midwestern, and eastern states see the most fires, but fires in the West are often larger and burn more land.

Temperatures Rising

Our planet is heating up quickly due to human activity. We burn **fossil fuels**—gas, oil, and coal—to create energy. This energy powers our cars, homes, and machines. But burning fossil fuels releases harmful gases, such as **carbon dioxide**, into the air. Then, the gases trap heat around the planet.

Global warming is beginning to change our **climate**, or usual weather patterns. In hot, dry places, the weather is getting even hotter and drier.

Since 1880, average temperatures worldwide have risen by 1.9 degrees Fahrenheit (1.1 degrees Celsius). In the last 40 years, the rate of warming has doubled. The 10 warmest years on record have happened since 2005.

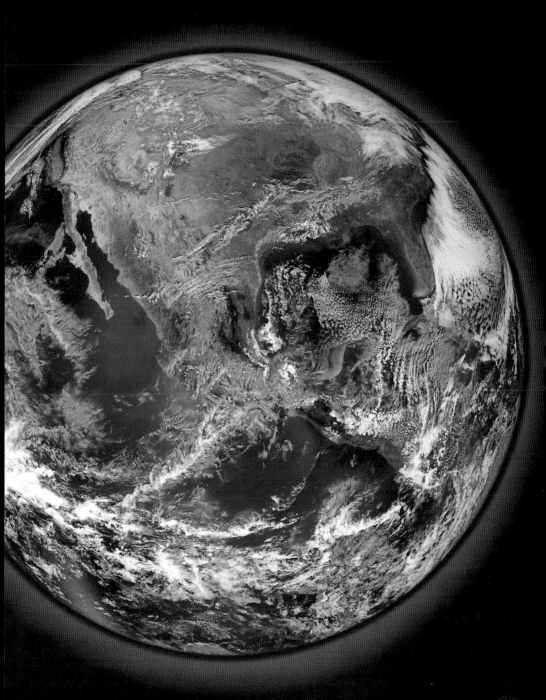

The gases that trap heat around Earth are known as greenhouse gases.

A Dry Heat

How does the mercury inching up make wildfires more likely? And why are these fires so dangerous? As temperatures rise, the warmer air acts like a sponge. It sucks **moisture** out of soil and **vegetation**. When plants and trees have enough water, they do not usually catch fire quickly. Fires that *do* start spread very slowly. But dried-out vegetation can light up at lower temperatures, and their flames burn hotter. These types of fires spread more quickly.

Wildfires make global climate change worse. Healthy trees, shrubs, and grasses remove heat-trapping carbon dioxide from the air. But when they burn, their stored carbon is released back into the air.

Water, Water Anywhere?

As our planet warms, some places are getting extra hot. Across the globe, there are more back-to-back hot days known as **heat waves**. The extreme heat paired with **droughts**— long periods with very little rainfall—dry out vegetation fast.

Flames can easily travel from one dried pile of brush to another and leap from dried tree to dried tree. Fires that break out in this way can spread so fast and far that they burn out of control quickly and keep going for a long time.

Since the 1970s, less rain has fallen in the western United States and droughts have lasted longer. During this time, there have been seven times as many fires, which have tripled the total area burned each year.

13

Melting Too Soon

A rainy spring and summer are the greatest protection against wildfires. But a snowy winter helps, too! The snow that piles up during the winter melts in the spring and summer. Melted snow can help keep the plants and soil damp during fire season.

But the same dry weather that causes droughts can lead to less snowfall. Because of warmer temperatures, this smaller amount of snow melts earlier in the spring. So, the soil and plants get this moisture sooner. In the hot, dry summer months when they really need moisture from melting snow, there is none left.

In 2020, snow cover in parts of California disappeared more than a month earlier than usual. The following wildfire season was the worst in state history. Almost 10,000 fires burned more than 4 percent of the state's land.

'Tis the Season

Hot temperatures, low rainfall, smaller **snowpacks**, and early melting are leading to drier conditions. At the same time, spring weather is coming earlier so vegetation is starting to dry out sooner than it used to. This means wildfires begin earlier and have more dry plants to burn. Autumn rains and cooler temperatures that end fire season now arrive later as well.

This shifting seasonal pattern means wildfires can start earlier and continue for several more weeks. As a result, fire seasons are getting longer.

The fire season in the western United States is more than 80 days longer than it was 50 years ago. In eastern Australia, it is almost 4 months longer than it was in the 1950s.

Beetle Baddies

One type of insect is enjoying the longer warm season that comes with global warming. Bark beetles are spreading across North America and Europe as temperatures rise. Milder winters are killing fewer of them. And the longer spring and summer seasons let bark beetles have even more time to **reproduce**.

Huge groups of bark beetles **invade** trees and chew on the bark. They lay their eggs in the holes they've made. The trees become home for baby beetles, but the damage to the bark can kill the plants. Dead, dried-out trees can make very hot wildfires that burn quickly.

Healthy trees create a sap that protects them from bark beetles. But during droughts, dry trees cannot make sap, so it is easier for beetles to dig paths through their bark.

Spark to a Flame

Our planet's trapped heat, rising temperatures, and bark beetles are creating lots of dry and dead vegetation to feed wildfires. But to start burning, fires need a spark.

Almost half of all wildfires in Canada and the western United States are caused by lightning. Lightning strikes lead to more fires more often in places that have been dried out. There, the air is so warm that rain can dry up and disappear before it even hits the ground. Then, when lightning strikes dried-out vegetation and starts a fire, no rain falls to help fight the flames.

In 2021, a wildfire in Oregon created a towering cloud of hot air and smoke that made its own lightning! The cloud rose as high as the flight paths used by passenger jets.

Caught in a Fire Trap

Wildfires not only destroy trees and plants, but also harm animals. Some animals, such as turtles and salamanders, can hide under rocks or bury themselves underground until fires burn themselves out. Birds and quick animals may be able to leave the area and find safety beyond the flames.

But slower, larger animals—such as bison, elk, and mountain lions—cannot always escape wildfires. Neither can very old or very young animals. They can be burned by the flames or breathe in too much deadly smoke.

Wildfires can destroy animals' homes and sources of food and water. So, even after a fire has burned itself out, some animals cannot return to their old homes.

Threatening Health and Home

The animals, trees, and plants that live in the path of wildfires are in great danger. And so are humans. Every year, thousands of homes and businesses burn to the ground around the world. Hundreds of people are killed.

Smoke from wildfires can rise 14 miles (22.5 km) into the sky, where wind can carry it around the globe. This smoke can make the air unsafe to breathe.

Wildfires in Russia have created smoky conditions in Alaska and Washington. Smoke from California wildfires has traveled across the country as far as New York and Washington, D.C.

Fighting Fire with Fire

It may sound strange, but the best way to prevent huge wildfires is to set smaller fires. Forest managers carefully start **controlled burns** to safely destroy the dry vegetation that could otherwise feed huge, uncontrolled wildfires. This also creates more space between trees, so flames can't easily jump between them. After the controlled fires are put out, the new plants that grow don't catch fire as easily. People around the world are finding equally exciting ways to improve our planet's health and protect all living creatures from fire.

In France, Greece, Italy, and Spain, wildfires have been reduced by letting animals **graze** in the forests. Sheep, goats, and cattle eat plants that could feed the flames.

Battle Wildfires!

The hotter, drier weather caused by global warming makes wildfires more likely and more damaging. Lightning is the leading natural cause of wildfires, but people being careless with matches, lighters, and campfires start most of these fires. You can help prevent fire with a few easy steps.

Don't start campfires during droughts or when it's dry and windy. Check for burn **bans** in your area before starting a fire.

Build fires a safe distance from trees or vegetation. Be sure there is a fire ring or circle of rocks around the fire's edge.

Keep a bucket of water near the fire at all times. Watch for flying embers that make their way out of the fire.

When you are finished, make sure your fire is completely out. Cover it with water. Stir it up with a shovel. Then, dump more water on it.

To make your home safer when wildfires are in the area, remove any dead trees, leaves, and dry brush from your yard and keep your plants and trees watered.

Glossary

bans rules that do not allow something

billowing rising up or rolling like waves

carbon dioxide a gas given off when fossil fuels are burned

climate the typical weather in a place

controlled burns fires that are intentionally set and controlled to prevent dangerous wildfires from causing damage

droughts long periods of time with dry weather

fire seasons the stretches of time during which fires are likely in an area

fossil fuels fuels such as coal, oil, and gas made from the remains of plants and other organisms that died millions of years ago

graze to eat grass or other vegetation

heat waves very hot weather that lasts for several days

invade to take over, usually in a harmful way

moisture water contained in something such as a cloud

reproduce to have young

snowpacks the piles of snow that collect in places, especially mountainous areas, during winter

vegetation different types of plants, including grasses, bushes, and trees

Read More

Buckley, James, Jr. *Wildfire Escape: Pet Animals Rescue! (Rescued! Animal Escapes).* Minneapolis: Bearport Publishing Company, 2021.

Hamilton, S. L. *Fleeing California Wildfires (Xtreme Rescues).* Minneapolis: Abdo, 2020.

McDaniel, Melissa. *Facing a Warming World (A True Book: Understanding Climate Change).* New York: Children's Press, 2020.

Minoglio, Andrea. *Our World Out of Balance: Understanding Climate Change and What We Can Do.* San Francisco: Blue Dot Kids Press, 2021.

Learn More Online

1. Go to **www.factsurfer.com** or scan the QR code below.

2. Enter "**Fires Everywhere**" into the search box.

3. Click on the cover of this book to see a list of websites.

Index

About the Author

Raymond Bergin is a writer living in New Jersey. In the summer of 2021, his neighborhood was blanketed by a smoky haze that had traveled almost 3,000 miles (4,828 km) from wildfires burning in the western United States and Canada.